The Most Deliciou[s]

from Walking Dead

The Best Cookbook for Apocalypse

By - Rene Reed

License Notes

Table of Contents

Introduction

Do you believe in the apocalypse? Do you think that zombies can take over the world at any time? Food is what you will need in the tough time and, too, with minimal ingredients.

This cookbook is a survival guide for all Walking Dead fans. You will get yummy recipes that are easy to cook. Zombies can survive on flesh and blood, but we need proper food to survive the apocalypse. Here is the highly exclusive cookbook that jumps in to save us.

You can adopt a unique way of celebrating any event with the Walking Dead theme to stand out in cute and flowery themed parties! Food is definitely the most important part of such parties, and our cookbook is really a lifesaver!

Halloween is an important celebration, and everyone needs yummy food for the event. The cookbook guides you to choose the scariest appetizers, main courses, and desserts. Pick any recipe of your choice and amaze your friends and family with your cooking skills.

Starters

Blood-shot Deviled Eggs

What could be scarier than the bloodshot eyes of zombies? If you are a fan of Walking Dead, you would love this recipe. It is so easy that you can make it in minutes. Let your kids show you some love by lending a hand in the kitchen.

Serving size: 8

Cooking time: 30 minutes

Ingredients:

- Hard-boiled eggs 8
- Fresh juiced lemon 1
- Beet juice 1 cup
- Black pepper 1/8 teaspoon
- Mayonnaise 3 tablespoons
- Halved green olives 8
- Salt ¼ teaspoon
- Dijon-style mustard 1 teaspoon

Instructions:

Heat beat juice in a small saucepan over high heat for 5 minutes until thickened.

Peel and halve all the eggs. Transfer all the egg yolks to a bowl and set egg whites aside.

Add lemon juice, mayonnaise, salt, pepper, mustard, and 1 tablespoon of beet juice to the egg yolks.

Mash the egg yolks until smooth. Add more beet juice if necessary.

Spoon an equal amount of egg yolk mixture into each egg white.

Transfer the eggs to the serving dish and place green olives in the center of each egg on top of the yolk mixture.

Take a small paintbrush and make small lines on the surface of egg whites with the remaining beet juice.

Chill the eggs until they are ready to serve.

Peanut Butter Mummy Pops

Mummies have strong connections with zombies as they also form corpses. Give your starters a yummy twist this Halloween, and make these fun pops. You can make them for a snack too.

Serving size: 48 mini pops

Cooking time: 2 hours 15 minutes

Ingredients:

- Creamy peanut butter 1 cup
- Sugar cookie mix 1 pouch
- Candy eyeballs 72
- Lollipop sticks 48
- Vanilla flavored candy coating 1 package

Instructions:

Preheat the oven to 350°F and make the cookie dough according to the package directions.

Make small balls of equal size from the cookie dough.

Transfer the balls to a cookie sheet and press the lollipop stick into half the cookie balls.

Bake for 10 minutes until edges are golden brown.

Spread peanut butter on cookies and cover with the remaining cookies making a sandwich.

Melt candy coating in an oven according to the package instructions.

Dip each cookie sandwich in the melted candy coating to coat completely.

Cool the cookie lollipops for 20 minutes.

Drizzle all the cookie lollipops with the remaining candy coating.

Press two candy eyeballs into each of the cookie lollipops and cool for 1 hour before serving.

Heaton's Tombstone and Coffin Grilled Cheese

Zombies come from the graveyard and celebrate a party with Walking Dead as the theme class for something from there. Grilled cheese will change its look as soon as you apply some creative garnishing skills to it.

Serving size: 8

Cooking time: 40 minutes

Ingredients:

- Shredded cheddar cheese 1 cup
- Fig jam ¼ cup
- Shredded gouda 1 cup
- Prepared pesto ¼ cup
- Shredded Monterey jack 1 cup
- Dark sandwich bread 8 slices
- Shredded mozzarella 1 cup
- Mustard ½ cup
- Unsalted butter ½ cup
- Thinly shredded iceberg lettuce 8 cups
- Ketchup ½ cup
- White sandwich bread 8 slices

Instructions:

Preheat the oven to 450°F.

Mix gouda, cheddar, Monterey Jack, and mozzarella in a bowl.

Spread the pesto and half of the cheese mixture evenly on the white bread slices.

Top with remaining slices to make sandwiches.

Line the baking sheet with parchment paper and transfer the white bread sandwiches.

Spread all of the fig jam on half of the slices of dark bread and the remaining amount of cheese mixture on the other half of the dark bread.

Transfer dark bread sandwiches to the baking tray and brush the top of the sandwiches with unsalted butter.

Bake the sandwiches for 8 minutes and flip the sides in the last 3 mins of baking.

For preparing tombstones, cut the crusts off the sides and curve the top surface of the white bread sandwiches.

Cut each sandwich in half using a knife.

For making coffins, remove the crusts of three sides of each dark bread sandwich.

Cut each sandwich to form two long rectangles.

Make aslant cuts at each corner of the coffin sandwich to give it a hexagonal shape.

Decorate the coffins and tombstones with mustard and ketchup.

Spread the shredded lettuce on a serving platter and hide coffins in the lettuce. Place the gravestones on top of the lettuce.

Bacon-Wrapped Jalapeno Ghouls

Use this recipe and see how your lovely, spicy, and hot jalapenos become these nasty, dreadful, and scary ghouls. The recipe is easy, and we bet you cannot find a better appetizer for your Waling Dead or Halloween party.

Serving size: 6

Cooking time: 35 minutes

Ingredients:

- Greek yogurt ¼ cup
- Finely grated Parmesan cheese ¼ cup
- Large jalapenos 4
- Dried thyme ½ teaspoon
- Pitted black olives 2
- Grainy mustard 1 teaspoon
- Bacon strips 4

Instructions:

Preheat the oven to 325°F.

Cut the jalapenos lengthwise and remove seeds and veins properly.

Combine Greek yogurt, dried thyme, grainy mustard, and parmesan cheese in a small bowl.

Line a baking sheet with aluminum foil and transfer the jalapenos.

Divide the cheese mixture evenly between jalapenos and smooth out the top.

Cut the bacon into thin strips and wrap the strips around jalapenos.

Cover and refrigerate for 10 minutes.

Bake for 15 minutes until melted cheese and crispy bacon.

Place two pieces of diced black olive on each stuffed jalapeno.

Serve warm. Enjoy!

Main courses

Venison Jerky

Meat is what we think will be available for food in the apocalypse. This recipe is easy to make, and you can store it for quite a long time. So, if you need to survive through a zombies' attack, learn this recipe and make it often for extra practice. Follow our recipe, and you will have the tastiest food in the disaster.

Serving size: 6

Cooking time: 35 minutes

Ingredients:

- Garlic powder ¼ teaspoon
- Boneless venison or beef 1 lb.
- Liquid smoke flavoring 1 tablespoon
- Onion powder ¼ teaspoon
- Soy sauce 4 tablespoons
- Salt 1 teaspoon
- Worcestershire sauce 2 tablespoons
- Pepper ¼ teaspoon

Instructions:

Preheat the oven or dehydrator to 165°F.

Wash the meat properly and slice it into thin pieces.

Combine soy sauce, garlic powder, Worcestershire sauce, onion powder, liquid smoke flavoring, pepper, and salt in a large releasable plastic bag.

Transfer the meat to the plastic bag.

Close the bag properly and refrigerate overnight.

Place the meat on the racks and dehydrate for 7 hours until meat breaks when trying to bend.

Huckleberry Grilled Doves

If you are on the run in forests to escape from zombies, you might have to starve. However, you can always find doves and other birds to survive. Here is a mouthwatering recipe to cook beautiful doves in the best way. Learn this recipe for difficult times, and use the same recipe for chicken thighs, which you can buy from the store in routine.

Serving size: 4

Cooking time: 45 minutes

Ingredients:

- Doves 16 or chicken thighs 2 lb.
- Cayenne pepper 1 teaspoon
- Minced rosemary 1 teaspoon
- Chopped onion ½ cup
- Tomato puree ½ cup
- Cider vinegar 1 cup
- Blueberries or huckleberries 2 cups
- Brown sugar ½ cup
- Dry mustard 2 teaspoons
- Chopped garlic cloves 2
- Unsalted butter 3 tablespoons
- Salt as per your taste
- Olive oil 2 tablespoons

Instructions:

Season the doves with salt generously.

For making the sauce, melt butter in a cooking pot over medium to high heat.

Sauté onions in the melted butter for 2 minutes and then garlic for 1 minute.

Add all the remaining ingredients to the cooking pot and simmer for 30 minutes.

Blend the sauce in a blender for 2 minutes until smooth.

Coat the doves with olive oil and place the breast side up on the grill.

Cover and grill for 2 minutes.

Pour half of the sauce all over the doves and grill for 10 minutes.

Transfer the doves to a serving platter and serve warm with the remaining sauce.

Special Zombies' Smoked Pheasant

Are you left all alone in the wilderness, and zombies are everywhere in the cities? Worry no more! Use stones or make-shift weapons to grab some pheasants in the wilderness. You may need a few basic utensils to follow our recipe. However, if zombies are around, setting up a fire is enough to cook these pheasants.

Serving size: 6

Cooking time: 3 hours 30 minutes

Ingredients:

- Whole pheasants 2
- Water 4 cups
- Kosher salt ¼ cup
- Maple syrup 2 cups
- Brown sugar ¼ cup

Instructions:

Dissolve sugar and kosher salt in the water.

Take a large lidded container and transfer pheasants.

Cover with the brine solution and set aside for 12 hours.

Take the pheasants out of the container and let them dry completely.

Smoke the pheasants over any wood of your choice for 3 hours.

Baste the pheasants with maple syrup after every 30 minutes.

Remove when pheasants reach an internal temperature of 160°F.

Baste with maple syrup before serving for rich flavor.

Hmong Squirrel Stew

Buying chopped chicken thighs and tender and juicy fillets is not the option if you have zombies all around. Availability of food is more important than choice. Squirrels are the best possible option for such times, and here is how you can convert them into a mouthwatering stew.

Serving size: 6

Cooking time: 2 hours 20 minutes

Ingredients:

- Squirrels 2
- Chicken stock 4 cups
- Ground Sichuan peppercorns 1 teaspoon
- Minced garlic cloves 4
- Minced white part of lemongrass 1 stalk
- Soy sauce 1 tablespoon
- Minced galangal 1 tablespoon
- Chopped Bok choy or Chard 1 lb.
- Peeled and minced ginger 2 tablespoons
- Lime juice 1 tablespoon
- Snow peas ¼ lb.
- Chopped green onion ½ cup
- Vegetable oil 3 tablespoons
- Chopped red chilis 4
- Salt as per your taste
- Chopped mint ½ cup
- Chopped cilantro ½ cup

Instructions:

Cut the squirrel into small pieces.

Next, heat the oil in a large pot over medium to high heat.

Cook squirrel in vegetable oil until browned evenly. Transfer the cooked squirrel pieces to the plate and set them aside.

Put ginger, garlic, galangal, chilis, and lemongrass in the cooking pot. Cook for 1 minute on medium to high heat.

Add soy sauce, chicken broth, lime juice, and squirrel to the cooking pot.

Then, cook for 1 to 2 hours until the meat is cooked properly.

Add snow peas, Bok choy, and shredded squirrel meat to the cooking pot and cook for 10 minutes.

Season with salt and Sichuan pepper.

Garnish with chopped mint, cilantro, and green onion before serving.

Moose Meatballs

If you are living in an area where you can find a moose easily, surviving an apocalypse is no more difficult then. Capture a moose, and let us guide you through making it into these drool-worthy meatballs. If you are making them for a Halloween party, serve them with your favorite side dish and enjoy them as the main course food.

Serving size: 4

Cooking time: 30 minutes

Ingredients:

- Ground moose meat 1 lb.
- Chopped onion 2 tablespoons
- Salt 1 teaspoon
- Beaten egg 1
- Canola oil 1 tablespoon
- Pepper ¼ teaspoon
- Pineapple chunks 1 cup
- Green pepper 1
- Cooked egg noodles 1 package
- Sugar ½ cup
- White vinegar 3 tablespoons
- Soy sauce 1 tablespoon
- Cornstarch 4 tablespoons
- Water 1 cup

Instructions:

Combine meat, pepper, egg, onion, and 1 tablespoon of cornstarch in a bowl.

Make small balls of even size and fry in oil over low heat for 10 minutes until they are cooked properly.

Mix vinegar and the remaining cornstarch until smooth.

Add sugar, soy sauce, and water to the cornstarch mixture. Cook over medium heat until thickened.

Put meatballs, pineapple chunks, and green pepper. Cook until heated and green pepper is tender.

Serve with noodles immediately.

Venison Tenderloins

Feel yourself extremely lucky if you find a deer for food in the apocalypse. This royal meal is fit for your formal dinners to give a luxurious touch. However, while surviving a zombie attack, eating a deer becomes a basic need. Use your bow and arrow or any other make-shift weapon to grab a deer from the wilderness and follow this recipe to cook these juicy, tender, and flavorful tenderloins.

Serving size: 8

Cooking time: 20 minutes

Ingredients:

- Venison tenderloin steaks 8
- Lemon juice 1/3 cup
- Soy sauce ¾ cup
- Minced garlic cloves 2
- Canola oil ½ cup
- Worcestershire sauce ¼ cup
- Ground mustard 2 tablespoons
- Dried parsley flakes 1 ½ teaspoons
- Red wine vinegar ½ cup
- Pepper 1 tablespoon

Instructions:

Mix all the ingredients in a deep shallow dish.

Put fillets in the shallow dish and turn to coat.

Cover and refrigerate the fillets for 7 hours or overnight.

Drain and discard marinade properly.

Grill each side of the fillet over medium heat for 4 minutes until the meat is done.

Serve warm.

Rabbit Gumbo

Rabbit meat is not a healthy option to survive because it has an extremely low amount of fat on it. However, to get some energy to find another source of food during an apocalypse, rabbit meat is a pretty good food item. Here is the perfect recipe to make rabbit gumbo for a yummy meal during the disaster.

Serving size: 6

Cooking time: 2 hours 25 minutes

Ingredients:

- Dressed rabbit 3 lb.
- Chopped green pepper 1
- Dried thyme ½ teaspoon
- Smoked sausage ½ lb.
- Cayenne pepper ¼ teaspoon
- Chopped onion 1
- Canola oil ¼ cup
- Salt 1 teaspoon
- Sliced okra ½ cup
- Pepper ¼ teaspoon
- Water as much required

Instructions:

In a Dutch oven, sauté green pepper and onion in oil until tender.

Cut the rabbit meat into pieces.

Put the rabbit in the Dutch oven and add enough water to cover the rabbit.

Cover and cook for 2 hours until the meat is properly done.

Cut sausages into 1/4 inch slices and transfer to the Dutch oven

Add cayenne, salt, thyme, pepper, and cook for 15 minutes.

Remove rabbit meat from bones and discard the bones.

Cut into small pieces and add okra. Cook for 3 minutes.

Serve warm with rice or any other meal of your choice.

Cavemen Elk Steaks

Did you ever wonder how cavemen used to cook before fancy stoves and lavish kitchens? With zombies all around, you need to find out the easiest possible way of cooking the available meat. Make these steaks to have a new flavor among beef and chicken steaks.

Serving size: 2

Cooking time: 40 minutes

Ingredients:

- Bone-in elk loin steaks 2
- Brown sugar 2 tablespoons
- Ground coffee 3 tablespoons
- Kosher salt 1 tablespoon
- Paprika ½ teaspoon
- Black pepper 3 tablespoons
- Cayenne ½ teaspoon

Instructions:

Mix all the ingredients in a bowl and season both sides of the steak generously.

Start a hardwood fire and place the steaks directly on the coal.

Cook each side of the steak for 5 minutes until the meat is properly cooked.

Remove the elk steak from the fire and brush away any ash.

Serve warm after slicing.

Roasted Chicken

Roasting a chicken is the easiest method of arranging food during an apocalypse. You can find chicken anywhere, maybe somewhere in a looted store or ruined courtyard. Get a chicken and use this recipe to roast it to perfection. Have fun at your family barbecue with it because you don't need to wait for zombies to take over to make the dish.

Serving size: 5

Cooking time: 1 hour 45 minutes

Ingredients:

- Whole chicken 4 lb.
- Olive oil 2 teaspoons
- Rosemary sprigs 3
- Salt 1 teaspoon
- Minced garlic cloves 3
- Finely chopped parsley 1 tablespoon
- Finely chopped sage 1 tablespoon
- Unsalted butter ½ cup
- Quartered lemon 1
- Pepper as per your taste
- Halved garlic bulb 1
- Chicken broth 1 cup
- Finely chopped rosemary 2 teaspoons
- Lemon juice 2 tablespoons

Instructions:

Preheat the oven to 450°F.

Discard neck from the chicken cavity.

Mix minced garlic, salt, parsley, pepper, butter, sage, chopped rosemary, and lemon juice in a small bowl.

Rub the chicken with more than half of the dressing until all the chicken is evenly coated.

Stuff the inside of the chicken with garlic bulb, quartered lemon, and rosemary sprigs.

Tie the chicken legs with a kitchen string properly.

Pour chicken broth all over the chicken.

Drizzle the chicken with olive oil in the end.

Transfer the chicken to the oven carefully and roast for 10 minutes.

Reduce the temperature to 350°F and roast the chicken for 1 hour and 15 minutes.

Remove the chicken from the oven and pour the remaining dressing all over the chicken.

Roast the chicken for 10 minutes more.

Hunter-Beef

Becoming a hunter is no more a matter of choice when you need for survival in a disaster like a zombies' attack. Ask your friends to join hands to find a big animal which is enough for all people around you. Hunter beef is the best way to cook meat with minimal ingredients. You may use this recipe for a cozy gathering with friends and family outdoor.

Serving size: 6

Cooking time: 10 hours 10 minutes

Ingredients:

- Beef carved in bread shape 3 Ib.
- Peeled garlic cloves 12
- Salt as per your taste
- Butter 3 tablespoons
- White vinegar 1 cup
- Black pepper 2 tablespoons
- Lemon juice ¼ cup
- Lemon wedges for serving

Instructions:

Prick all around the beef with a sharp knife.

Place a garlic clove into each hole.

Mix white vinegar, pepper, lemon juice, and salt in a bowl.

Pour the mixture all over the beef and cover it with a plastic bag.

Marinate the beef for at least 8 hours.

Put the marinated beef in steamer and steam for 35 minutes.

Bake the steamed beef in an oven for 20 minutes until cooked properly.

Serve with lemon wedges and any sauce of your choice.

Roasted Turkey

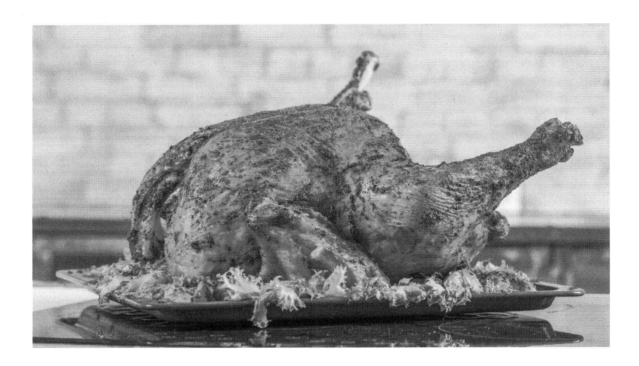

There are high chances that you get a turkey in the wilderness while running for life from zombies. The basic thing you will need to cook this dish is turkey. All of its ingredients are the most basic if you are cooking it in your kitchen. You are welcome to cook your turkey with this recipe for the coming festive season.

Serving size: 8

Cooking time: 3 hours

Ingredients:

- Fresh turkey 10 lb.
- Lemon zested and juiced 1
- Quartered Spanish onion 1
- Black pepper as per your taste
- Chopped thyme leaves 1 teaspoon
- Unsalted butter ½ cup
- Halved garlic head 1
- Kosher salt as per your taste
- Halved lemon 1
- Bunch of fresh thyme 1

Instructions:

First, preheat the oven to 350°F.

Second, melt butter in a saucepan over low to medium heat.

Next, add thyme leaves, lemon juice, and lemon zest to the butter mixture.

Clean and remove any excess fat from the turkey.

Transfer the turkey to a large roasting pan.

Season the inside and outside surface of the turkey with salt and pepper generously.

Stuff the inside of the turkey cavity with lemon, onion, thyme, and garlic.

Next, brush the outside surface of the turkey with the butter mixture.

Then, tie the legs together with the help of kitchen string.

Roast the turkey for 2 ½ hours until cooked properly.

Serve warm after slicing.

Beef Steaks

With zombies roaming around, there is no time to grow any food crops, and the only food option left is meat. Here is a recipe which you will prize the most from our collection. This beef steak recipe is the easiest one, but the cooking steps are extremely special. The recipe is so simple that you can easily manage it even during the apocalypse.

Serving size: 4

Cooking time: 30 minutes

Ingredients:

- Tenderloin beef steak 4
- Pepper ¼ teaspoon
- Salt 1 teaspoon

Instructions:

Heat the gas grill for 10 minutes.

Place the steaks on the grill rack over medium heat.

Cover the grill. Then, cook for 15 minutes until the meat is properly done.

Flip the sides of the steak in the midway of cooking.

Season the steaks with salt and pepper. Serve warm

Bean and Beef Casserole

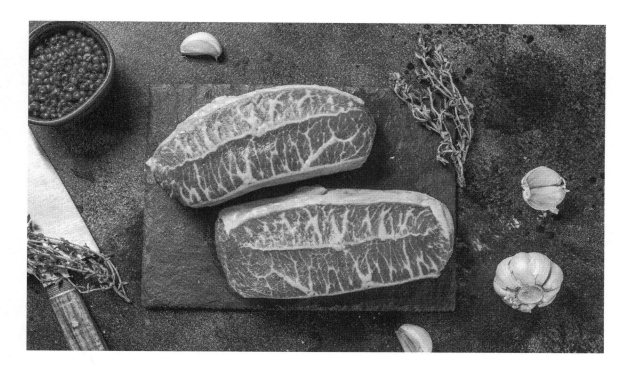

Wild beans and meat are a good food option when you are no more in-home and need food for survival. This dish is sophisticated enough to be a part of our special Walking Dead parties. Make it for Halloween, and you are ready to impress your family and friends.

Serving size: 4

Cooking time: 2 hours 25 minutes

Ingredients:

- Beef chuck steak 1 ½ lb.
- Crushed garlic cloves 2
- Olive oil 2 tablespoons
- Chopped thyme sprigs 4
- Thin sliced leek 1
- Red wine ½ cup
- Tomato paste 2 tablespoons
- Salt as per your taste
- Crushed tomatoes 1 ½ cups
- Thin sliced celery sticks 2
- Beef stock 1 cup
- Peeled and thick-sliced carrot 1
- Cannellini beans 1 ½ cups
- Pepper as per your taste

Instructions:

Cut the beef steak into small pieces.

Next, heat olive oil in a large saucepan over low to medium heat.

Cook the beef in a saucepan until all sides are evenly browned.

Transfer the cooked beef to a plate and set it aside.

Add carrot, garlic, leek, and celery to the same saucepan and cook for 5 minutes.

Put beef, tomato paste, salt, beef stock, thyme, pepper, tomato, beans, and wine.

Then, reduce the heat to low. Cook for 2 hours until beef is cooked properly.

Taste and season with more salt and pepper if necessary.

Transfer the beans and beef casserole to the serving bowls. Serve warm.

Venison Kebabs

If you are lucky enough to get your hands on a deer, these venison kebabs are what you can make out of them. Again, the ingredients are simple, readily available, and you are welcome to delete any of them if you want to. This recipe is perfect to be used with beef, mutton or any type of meat.

Serving size: 4

Cooking time: 45 minutes

Ingredients:

- Venison steak 1 lb.
- Olive oil 2 tablespoons
- Mushrooms 8
- Pepper as per your taste
- Jerk spice 2 tablespoons
- Peeled red onion 1
- Thin sliced courgette 1
- Yellow pepper
- Salt as per your taste

Instructions:

Cut the venison steak into cubes.

Transfer the venison cubes to a bowl and add jerk spice.

Mix properly to evenly coat the cubes with jerk spice.

Cut the courgette into thin slices

Cut the red onion into wedges and yellow pepper into small bite-sized chunks.

Thread the meat and all the vegetables onto the wooden skewers.

Season the kebabs with salt and pepper.

Brush the kebabs with olive oil.

Grill each side of kebabs for 7 minutes until meat is cooked properly.

Serve with a salad or any other barbecue side dish.

Whole Rainbow Trout

Living in the wilderness will get you all-natural food in abundance. Trout lives in freshwater, and there are fair chances of you catching a few of it. Otherwise, buy trout from the market, and this recipe will yield the most tender, juicy, and aromatic trout you have ever tasted.

Serving size: 4

Cooking time: 30 minutes

Ingredients:

- Gutted trout 3 lb.
- Cold butter 2 tablespoons
- Rosemary sprig 1
- Garlic cloves 3
- Lemon juice 1
- Lemon slices 5
- Salt 1 teaspoon
- Chopped thyme sprigs 2
- Black pepper 1 ½ teaspoon
- Pearled barley salad 2 cups
- Chopped parsley 1 tablespoon
- Clarified butter 3 tablespoons
- Red pepper flakes 1 teaspoon
- Thyme sprigs 2
- Extra virgin olive oil 2 tablespoons

Instructions:

Preheat the oven to 450°F.

Stuff the trout with pepper, thyme, lemon, salt, and rosemary sprigs.

Melt the clarified butter in a large pan over medium heat.

Transfer the trout to the pan and cook for 10 minutes until both sides are browned.

Transfer the trout to a plate and set it aside.

Add cold butter, garlic, chopped thyme, and red pepper flakes to the pan. Cook for 1 minute.

Spoon the butter mixture over the trout.

Serve the stuffed trout over pearled barley salad.

Drizzle the trout with lemon juice, oil, and chopped herbs if desired.

Wild Harvest Pie

During an apocalypse, food can be your biggest survival question. If meat is not available, you need to learn to find edible plants, herbs, and grains. This recipe does not contain any type of meat, and you need all of the ingredients from plants.

Serving size: 2

Cooking time: 55 minutes

Ingredients:

- Baked pie shells 2
- Butter ¼ cup
- Finely chopped apples 3 cups
- Organic cane sugar ½ cup
- Ground nutmeg ¼ teaspoon
- Spelt flour ½ cup
- Finely chopped cranberries 2 cups
- Ground cinnamon 4 teaspoons
- Chopped pecans 1/3 cup
- Brown sugar 1/3 cup
- Finely chopped elderberries 2 cups

Instructions:

Preheat the oven to 375°F.

Mix all the fruits in the bowl.

Add cane sugar, ground nutmeg, half of the cinnamon, and spelt flour to the fruit and mix properly.

Transfer the fruit mixture to baked pie shells.

Mix softened butter, brown sugar, the remaining portion of cinnamon, and spelt flour in a bowl.

Add pecans once the mixture is fully blended.

Place the pecans mixture on top of the fruit mixture.

Bake for 35 minutes until the topping is golden brown and the fruit is tender.

Serve warm with whipped cream or ice cream if desired.

Handmade Stinging Nettle Pasta

We crave our favorite food when we can't enjoy them anymore. Finding enough food to keep you alive is an achievement when flesh-eater zombies surround you. No need to worry if you can't have pasta on the run for survival. Here is a unique recipe of pasta for die-hard fans of Walking Dead.

Serving size: 2

Cooking time: 45 minutes

Ingredients:

- Blanched Nettle leaves 1 ½ cups
- All-purpose flour 2 cups
- Egg 1
- Sea salt ¼ teaspoon
- Minced ramp bulbs 2
- Dry white wine 1 tablespoon
- Butter 2 tablespoons
- De-stemmed and sliced shiitake mushrooms 2 cups
- Crushed red pepper ¼ tablespoon
- Parmesan cheese ¼ cup
- Half and half ½ cup
- Salted water 20 cups
- Salt ½ teaspoon

Instructions:

Put egg and Nettle in a food processor until smooth puree forms.

Add flour and sea salt to the nettle puree. Mix properly until the right consistency.

Make a ball from the dough and knead until elastic and smooth.

Wrap the dough with a plastic sheet and refrigerate in the fridge for 30 minutes.

Roll out and cut in any shape according to your choice using a pasta machine

Add 15 to 20 cups of salted water to a cooking pot and bring it to boil.

Put nettle pasta in the boiling water and cook for 3 minutes.

Drain the nettle pasta and toss it with butter.

Sauté ramps and crushed red pepper in butter over medium heat.

Cook for 2 minutes and then add mushrooms.

Cook the mushrooms until it starts to release the juices.

Add dry white wine, salt, and half and half to the cooking pot.

Cook for 2 minutes until thickened.

Put nettle pasta and toss to combine.

Taste the pasta and add more half and half if it is too dry.

Serve with freshly grated parmesan cheese.

Goat Cheese Stuffed Hibiscus Blossoms

Settling up after the apocalypse ends is a phase when you are getting all of the beauties of your life back. These are the days when the goats you have been farming are giving you milk to make cheese, and your hibiscus plants are blooming. Use both of the ingredients to make this pleasant looking dish which is a treat for eyes and taste buds simultaneously.

Serving size: 12

Cooking time: 40 minutes

Ingredients:

- Hibiscus or Rose Sharon flowers 12
- Beaten egg 1
- White flour 1 cup
- Pepper as per your taste
- Cream 2 tablespoons
- Garlic 4 teaspoons
- Goat cheese ½ cup
- Bread crumbs 1 ½ cups
- Salt as per your taste
- Finely chopped chive 1 ½ tablespoons

Instructions:

Rinse hibiscus flowers well to remove any insects. Set aside to dry.

Mix chopped chives in the goat cheese. Season with salt, garlic, and pepper.

Roll a teaspoon of goat cheese in your hand and form small balls of oval shape.

Place one ball of goat cheese in each flower and close the petals properly.

Add cream to the already beaten egg and mix properly.

Dip each stuffed flower in the egg mixture and then in flour to evenly coat.

Dip again in the egg mixture and then roll each flower in the breadcrumbs.

Transfer the flower carefully to a greased baking tray.

Bake at 350°F for 20 minutes until golden brown.

Mustard Marinated Chicken

To welcome better days again, a celebration is important. Invite your kith and kin and have a feast. This special chicken recipe is to uplift your mood and is rich enough to remind you that bad days are over. Make it once, and you will love to have it in every special meal.

Serving size: 6

Cooking time: 8 hours 20 minutes

Ingredients:

- Boneless and skinless chicken breast halves 6
- White vinegar ¼ cup
- Light brown sugar ½ cup
- Olive oil 6 tablespoons
- Lemon juice 1 ½ tablespoons
- Spicy brown mustard 3 tablespoons
- Black pepper as per your taste
- Minced garlic cloves 3
- Salt 1 ½ teaspoons

Instructions:

Mix white vinegar, garlic, sugar, salt, spicy brown mustard, and lemon juice in a small bowl.

Add pepper and olive oil and cover the chicken completely with the marinade.

Cover and refrigerate the chicken for 8 hours.

Remove the chicken and discard the marinade.

Grill each side of the chicken on a lightly greased grill for 10 minutes.

Serve warm after slicing.

Desserts

Blood Splatter Cookies

Blood and flesh are what zombies eat after. We took inspiration from the most horrible situation and recreated this recipe. The cookies are perfect for sending as Halloween goodies or serving at Halloween parties. You can also use them for Walking Dead inspired parties.

Serving size: 35 cookies

Cooking time: 3 hours 25 minutes

Ingredients:

- Unsalted butter 1 cup
- Plain flour 2 cups
- Vanilla extract 1 tablespoon
- Lemon juice 1 tablespoon
- Egg whites 2
- Caster sugar 1 cup
- Icing sugar 2 cups
- Red food coloring gel as much required
- Beaten egg 1
- Coldwater 1 tablespoon

Instructions:

Cream together the caster sugar, vanilla extract, and butter using an electric mixer until fluffy.

Add egg in the butter mixture and beat until combined well.

Put the flour and mix with a wooden spoon until it forms a dough.

Knead the dough gently and divide it into two portions of equal size.

Roll the dough and refrigerate for 1 hour.

Beat egg whites, icing sugar, and lemon juice for 5 minutes until stiff peaks form.

Add cold water gradually until soft peaks form.

Take 6 tablespoons of the icing and add red food coloring gel. Cover with the cling film.

Cover the remaining icing in a bowl with cling film

Make 35 small circles from the dough using a cookie cutter.

Chill the cookie circles for 15 minutes.

Preheat the oven to 375°F.

Transfer the cookies to a baking tray lined with baking paper.

Bake for 10 minutes until the edges are golden. Flip the sides of the cookie after 5 minutes of baking.

Spread the icing on each cookie and decorate with red food color icing. Leave the cookies to set for 2 hours.

Elderberry Syrup

Desserts imply sweetness, which in turn means happiness. Bring some touch of sweetness and happiness in the mid of the apocalypse with this unique sweet recipe. The best thing is that it will heal all of your sore throats and coughs. With no particular medical aid around, make this delight for hitting two birds with one stone.

Serving size: 6 cups

Cooking time: 40 minutes

Ingredients:

- Water 6 cups
- Usnea 1 cup
- Fresh elderberries 2 cups
- Lemon juice 3 tablespoons
- Echinacea flowers 1 cup
- Sliced turkey tail mushrooms 1 cup
- Honey 1 cup
- Finely chopped ginger 3 tablespoons

Instructions:

Mix all the ingredients except lemon juice and honey in a saucepan.

Cook for 40 minutes over low heat.

Remove the saucepan from the heat and strain out the herbs.

Add honey and lemon juice to the syrup.

Transfer the syrup to jars and bottles.

Refrigerate the syrup, and it can be used for up to 3 months.

Pull-Apart Graveyard Cupcakes

Make your Halloween spookier with these yummy but dreadful-looking cupcakes. The chocolate, pumpkin and candy bring a festive touch to the mini treat. You must make them in big batches to share with your loved ones too.

Serving size: 12

Cooking time: 2 hours

Ingredients:

- Chocolate sandwich cookies with white filling 12
- Chocolate-flavor candy coating discs 1/3 cup
- Candy pumpkins 12
- Canned creamy white frosting 1 ½ cups
- Cream cupcakes 12

Instructions:

Split the chocolate sandwich cookies in half and remove the white filling.

Cut half of the cookies to make a tombstone shape using a serrated knife.

Crush the remaining cookies and transfer the ¼ cup of the creamy white frosting to a resealable plastic bag.

Snip off a small piece from the corner of a plastic bag and write RIP, BOO, or other messages on the flat sides of the tombstone cookies.

Heat the chocolate candy coating discs in a microwave for 30 seconds.

Transfer the candy coating to a resealable plastic bag and snip off a small piece from the corner.

Place a sheet of waxed paper on a baking tray and make 12 small leafless trees.

Chill in the refrigerator until the chocolate tree hardens.

Top the cupcakes with white creamy frosting generously and insert a cookie tombstone into each of the cupcakes.

Remove chocolate trees from the waxed paper carefully and place one tree on each of the cupcakes.

Place pumpkin candy on top of the cupcakes and sprinkle the crushed cookies on each cupcake.

Serve immediately or chill for later. Enjoy!

Patricia Heaton's Zombie Punch

The look of this recipe is enough to make it on top of the special Halloween menu this year. The perfect blend of yummy, juicy and fresh fruit will bring color to the darkness of your Walking Dead parties. Give it a try for an aromatic addition to your festive menu.

Serving size: 10

Cooking time: 4 hours 30 minutes

Ingredients:

- Whole lychees 4
- Pineapple juice 5 cups
- Oranges 4
- Blueberries 8
- Ginger ale 2 cups
- Vodka 2 cups
- Frozen strawberries 2 cups
- Triple sec liqueur 1 cup

Instructions:

Cut and discard the top quarter of each orange and hollow out the oranges reserving the orange pulp in a small bowl.

Place two blueberries and one lychee in the bottom of each orange and secure it with a toothpick.

Make at least 8 small cuts along the edges of the orange and fold every other cut to form eyelashes.

Transfer the oranges to the cups of muffin tin carefully and fill each orange with pineapple juice.

Freeze the oranges for 4 hours until solid and make sure to remove the toothpicks after some time.

For preparing the punch, blend strawberries and reserved orange pulp with triple sec and vodka until blended well.

Add pineapple juice and ginger ale to the strawberry mixture. Mix well.

Place the solid orange eyeballs carefully in the punch.

Maple Bourbon Pecan Pie

Carol is a skilled cook, and we can expect every type of gourmet wonders. This recipe suits her style, and we can imagine it laying somewhere around her. Our gourmet experts have recreated the recipe for you to savor while reliving the memories from your favorite movie.

Serving size: 6

Cooking time: 45 minutes

Ingredients:

- 9-inch pie shell 1
- Bourbon 2 tablespoons
- Milk ¾ cup
- Eggs 3
- Vanilla extract 2 teaspoons
- Unsalted butter ¼ cup
- Brown sugar 1 ¾ cups
- Toasted pecans 2 ½ cups
- Salt ½ teaspoon
- Maple syrup ½ cup

Instructions:

Whisk eggs and milk properly until blended.

Add salt, bourbon, brown sugar, maple syrup, butter, and vanilla extract. Whisk all the ingredients until combined well.

Put toasted pecans in the mixture and transfer to the pie shell carefully.

Bake the pie at 400°F for 10 minutes.

Reduce the temperature to 325°F and bake for 30 minutes more until the top is golden.

Serve warm after slicing.

Milk and Honey Ice Cream

Imagine the taste of organic wild honey! You will most probably find it somewhere in the wilderness while escaping from zombies. Milk is another ingredient you can get even during the worst days on planet earth. This recipe uses milk and honey as the main ingredients, and you can't forget the taste of this special ice cream.

Serving size: 8

Cooking time: 4 hours 50 minutes

Ingredients:

- Whole milk 3 cups
- Kosher salt ¾ teaspoon
- Heavy cream 1 cup
- Granulated sugar ½ cup
- Acacia honey 2 tablespoons
- Nonfat dry milk powder ¾ cup
- Unsalted butter 3 tablespoons
- Cornstarch 2 ½ teaspoons
- All-purpose flour 3 ½ tablespoons

Instructions:

First, pour two cups of the milk into a saucepan and boil over low heat for 30 minutes.

Transfer the milk to a blender and add heavy cream, 1 tablespoon of honey, ½ teaspoon of salt, ½ cup of dry milk powder, 1/3 cup of the granulated sugar, and the remaining milk.

Next, blend all the ingredients at high speed for 2 minutes.

Transfer the batter to a bowl and chill for at least 4 hours or overnight.

Preheat oven to 275°F.

For making milk crumble, combine butter and all the remaining ingredients in a small bowl.

Then, transfer the mixture to a baking tray and smooth out the top with a spoon.

Bake the milk crumble for 10 minutes in the oven.

Scoop ice cream and drizzle with the remaining honey.

Serve with milk crumble. Enjoy!

Spooky Witch Fingers

Add dreadfulness to the maximum to the food you have planned to cook this Halloween. These spooky fingers will drive your guests crazy regardless of age. The eerie green color and décor are enough to impress everyone around you.

Serving size: 28 cookies

Cooking time: 40 minutes

Ingredients:

- Unsalted butter 1 cup
- Almond extract 1 teaspoon
- Baking powder 1 teaspoon
- Whole blanched almonds ¾ cup
- Vanilla extract 1 teaspoon
- Powdered sugar 1 cup
- All-purpose flour 2 ¾ cups
- Green food coloring drops 4-6
- Salt 1 teaspoon
- Egg 1

Instructions:

Beat egg, vanilla extract, sugar, baking powder, almond extract, flour, salt, and butter in a small bowl.

Add green food coloring drops and refrigerate the dough for 30 minutes

Roll the dough and make finger-shaped cookies.

Press an almond into the end of each cookie for the nail part of the finger.

Transfer the cookies to a lightly greased baking tray carefully.

Bake at 325°F for 25 minutes in the oven.

Conclusion

This unique cookbook is meant for a range of readers and cooks. Walking Dead is a popular movie with zombies and apocalypse as the prime focus. If you are a fan of Walking Dead and want to throw a party with the same theme, the cookbook is all you need.

There are many people out there who believe that the apocalypse is real, and you need to practice survival during it beforehand. The cookbook contains a range of delicious food that you can make with easily available, simple, and minimal ingredients.

Since Halloween also involves zombies, the cookbook helps all enthusiastic celebrators to arrange special Halloween parties. You can also find a few things to prepare and share as a token of love with your loved ones too!

About the Author

Contemporary Caribbean cuisine had never tasted so good before Rene Reed came into the scene. With about twenty years dedicated to building up a budding culinary career, Rene has worked in various top-end restaurants, hotels, and resorts as the head chef. Her dive into the food industry started in Michigan, where she trained with some of the best chefs on the block. Rene was an accountant at a top firm but didn't feel a sense of accomplishment at the end of the day. Something was missing, and although Rene didn't know it at that time, the answer was right under her nose.

She discovered how relaxed and happy she felt when she was trying to whip up something in the kitchen for her family. To her, cooking was equivalent to vacation time, where she could do whatever she wanted. Encouraged by her family and loved ones, Rene quit her job and started her culinary training in earnest. Her efforts yielded so much success as she built up a network that propelled her to key positions all around the industry.

She specializes in exceptional Caribbean cuisine while also adding that unique Rene touch to every menu as much as she can.

Author's Afterthoughts

Thank you for taking out time to read my work. I put in all those hours, and I'm super glad that you found it worthy enough to download. I would love to ask for one more thing, and that is your feedback. It will be lovely to know your thoughts on the contents of the book. Was it worth your time? Would you like me to change anything for my subsequent books? I'll love to hear them all.

Thanks!

Rene Reed

Printed in Great Britain
by Amazon

61096139R00052